بِسْمِ ٱللَّهِ ٱلرَّحْمَـٰنِ ٱلرَّحِيمِ

Assalamu Alaykum wa Rahmat Allah wa Barakatuh,

Dear Reader,

One of the best acts of worship in Islam is reciting the Quran beautifully and smoothly.

The Prophet (Salla Allahu Alaihi wa Sallam) said:

"Verily the one who recites the Qur'an beautifully, smoothly, and precisely, he will be in the company of the noble and obedient angels. And as for the one who recites with difficulty, stammering or stumbling through its verses, then he will have TWICE that reward." [Al-Bukhari and Muslim]

Ever since teaching Quran to non Arabic speaking students, I realised the need to write a manual which would equip the students to recite the holy Quran beautifully and smoothly.

Janat Al Quran books aim to make learning the Quran easy for all students whether adults or children, beginners or advanced level. The books explain the Tajweed rules in English while the terms remain in Arabic with a translation for each term.

The books explain the Tajweed rules according to the narration of Hafs from the Imam Asem in the way of Ash-Shaatibiyah.

My sincere thanks go to my teachers who have taught me the science of Tajweed and the Quran recitation in the ten Qira'at. Special thanks to my sisters in Islam who helped me to enhance the books.

Message to the students:
Learning the Quran with a qualified teacher is of paramount importance. Correct recitation of the Quran can only be achieved through regular practice of the Quran with a teacher who can correct the mistakes.

Reciting the Quran on a daily basis is essential so the student can correct the mistakes pointed out by the teacher. Regular duas and patience are important to make your Quran journey easy and full of Barakah.

Message to the teachers:
Kindly be reminded to always renew your intention for teaching the Quran and to ensure the work is done solely for Allah's sake. It is important that we always motivate the students and inspire them to love the Quran.

May Allah Subhanahu wa Ta'la accept all our good deeds to please Him. May Allah unite us all in Jannah with his prophet Salla Allahu Alaihi wa Sallam.

Dina Essam

What some Shaykhs and teachers have said about the book

The Quran is the word of Allah which was revealed to the heart of the prophet SAW with an Arabic tongue. It was revealed Muratal (recited beautifully with Tajweed), that is the way it should always be recited and listened to so the listener can be in the beautiful Jannah of the Quran.

Jannat Al Quran books is a fantastic attempt from Shaykha Dina to get the reciter reach the Jannah of the Quran in order to make the Quran a path to the Firdaws in the hereafter in Shaa Allah. The Tajweed rules are explained with simplicity and clarity for anyone to understand. May Allah SWT reward the author of the book and the learners of the Quran.

Shaykh Samir Abd-Alazeem
Al-Azhar University

I would like to thank Shaykha Dina Essam for this great effort. We have always acknowledged this Khair and hard work from her in serving Allah's religion and His holy book.

I have read Jannat Al Quran books and found a good organisation for all the books and an easy explanation for all the Tajweed rules. Having all the Tajweed rules in those set of books makes the reader or the knowledge seeker who has learned the rules able to recite the Quran precisely with Allah's will. May Allah grant you success.

Shaykh Tamer Ibrahim,
Al-Azhar University

What some Shaykhs and teachers have said about the book

In the name of Allah who has revealed the holy book. I ask Allah to grant success to everyone who serves His religion, and give Barakah to Janat Al Quran books, this great work, that serves Allah's book.

These books give the chance to non Arabic speakers to understand the science of Tajweed of His book, for what they contain of valuable knowledge and simple method of explanation.

Sincere thanks to those who have helped in getting this book to the light in this way that is suitable for serving Allah's book.

I ask Allah to grant success to the writer and the learners of these books. May Allah grant Hidayah (guidance) to people through the learners of His book and may they become the best of people as the prophet said, "The best among you are those who learn the Qur'an and teach it.".

Mostafa Ibrahim
Al-Azhar University

The structure of Jannat Al Quran books will allow the student to successfully study the highly complex science of tajweed with simplicity. I would recommend it for sure!

Ayah Yussuf Teama
Al-Azhar University

Table of Contents

Table of Contents

First Section

Points of Articulation of
the Arabic letters
(Makhaarij) مَخَارِجُ الْحُرُوفِ الْعَرَبِيّة

How do humans produce sound?

The Speech System

Jannat
Al Quran

Points of Articulation of the Arabic letters
(Makhaarij) مَخَارِجُ الْحُرُوفِ الْعَرَبِيَّة

Arabic is a unique language in which each letter has a certain point of articulation مَخْرَج from where it is pronounced and cannot be pronounced from any other point of articulation. If the letter is not pronounced from the correct point of articulation مَخْرَج then the sound of the letter is incorrect. It can then be confused with one of the other letters.

This is why we should be careful when it comes to reciting the Quran, as changing the letter changes the meaning of the Ayah.

Example:

The word قَلْبٌ means heart, the word كَلْبٌ means dog. So if you change ق to ك the meaning will change.

What is the purpose of learing the Makhaarij of the Arabic language?

The purpose of learning the Makhaarij of the Arabic language is to make the reciter proficient in reciting the Qur'an by observing the correct pronunciation of every letter, without any exaggeration or deficiency. Through this, the reciter can recite the Qur'an according to the way of the prophet peace be upon him who received it from Jibreel who received it from Allah Subhanahu wa Ta'la in the classical Arabic language.

Points of Articulation of the Arabic letters (Makhaarij) مَخَارِجُ الْحُرُوفِ الْعَرَبِيّة

Definitions:

The articulation point: الْمَخْرَجُ
It is the place from where a letter is pronounced, making its sound different from the sound of other letters. Using the right articulation point of a letter is necessary to utter the letter correctly.

The sound: الْصَوْتُ
It is a group of vibrations and waves carried in the air to the human ears.

The letter: الْحَرْفُ
It is a sound that is pronounced from a specific articulation point.

To know the point of articulation of any letter, put a hamzah before the letter. For example if you want to know the point of articulation of the letter ب, put hamzah before it أَبْ .

If the Quran reader pronounces each letter from its proper articulation point, with all of the letter's characteristics, and can read each letter properly by itself, and in conjunction with other words, he has then achieved high quality in reading the Quran.

How do humans produce sound?

As we exhale, the air exits the lungs and creates an airstream which makes the vocal chords in the larynx vibrate. These vibrations then travel through the air to the human ears, where they are transformed into sounds.

How do humans produce 28 different sounds in the Arabic alphabet, using only 2 vocal chords?

The speech system is divided into five major areas. Each letter has one articulation point, which is used to produce the sound of the letter.

Some articulation points have more than one spot which produces different sounds. There are 17 different articulation points to pronounce the 28 Arabic letters and the Madd letters.

For a letter to be pronounced, there has to be a collision of two parts of the speech system. However this is not the case for the Madd letters, where you will have to create a distance to the colliding parts.

The Speech System

The following are the five major areas of the speech system:

1- The empty space in the mouth and throat: It has one articulation point for the three letters of Madd.

2- The Throat: It has three articulation points for six different letters which are pronounced from the deepest, middle, and closest part of the throat.

3- The Tongue: It has ten articulation points for eighteen letters.

4- The Two Lips: The lips have two articulation points for four letters.

5- The Nasal Cavity: It is a large air-filled space above and behind the nose, in the middle of the face. It is the continuation of both nostrils. There is one articulation point, that of the Ghunnah.

The Speech System

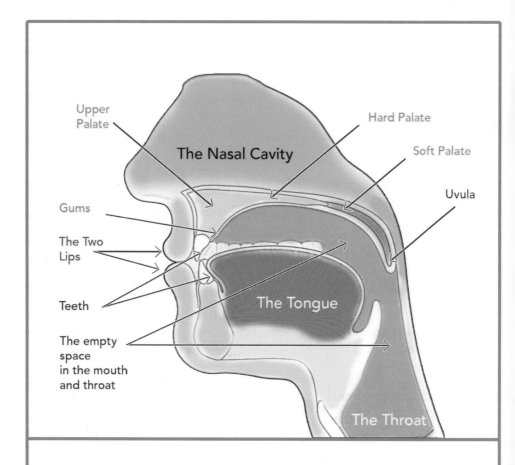

The points of articulation of the Arabic letters

will be explained in detail.

Second Section

The empty space in the throat and mouth (Al-Jawf) الْجَوْف

The Throat

The Tongue

The Lips

The Nasal Cavity

Jannat
Al Quran

The empty space in the throat and mouth (Al-Jawf) الْجَوْف

The empty space in the mouth and throat is a major area and an articulation point at the same time. The three Madd (lengthened) letters originate from this general area, these letters are:

• Waaw Sakinah preceded by a Dhammah
• Yaa Sakinah preceded by a Kasrah
• Alif preceded by a Fathah. (1)

These three Madd letters do not have a specific place that they are pronounced from, unlike all the other letters. Their sound is produced from the point of articulation of the previous letter.

When pronouncing the Alif, the sound should be rising. If the Alif is preceded by a heavy letter, the Alif should be heavy, whilst if preceded by a light letter, it will be light. Example: بَابٌ - طَالَ

When pronouncing the Waaw, the sound should be straight (neither falling nor rising), in addition to circling of the lips. (2) Example: يَفْعَلُونَ

When pronouncing the Yaa, the sound should be falling, in addition to raising of the middle part of the tongue.

Example: عَلِيمٌ

Note (1): Alif is always preceded by a fathah.
(2): The sound should come from the mouth not the nose.

6

The empty space in the throat and mouth (Al-Jawf) الْجَوْف

The Madd letters are prolonged two harakas if they are not followed by a hamzah or a sukoon.

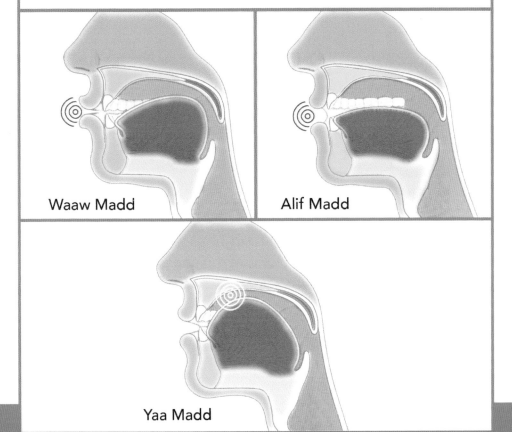

Waaw Madd

Alif Madd

Yaa Madd

The empty space in the throat and mouth (Al-Jawf) الْجَوْف

Common mistakes:

1- Pronouncing the Alif heavy where it should be light.

Examples: النَّهَارِ-النَّارِ

2- Pronouncing the Alif light where it should be heavy.

Examples: خَالِدِينَ-غَائِبَةٍ

3- Not emphasising the Dhammah on the letter before the Waaw Madd, when pronouncing the Waw Madd.

Example: يَعْمَلُونَ

4- Not emphasising the Kasrah on the letter before the Yaa Madd, when pronouncing the Yaa Madd.

Example: نَسْتَعِينُ

5- Pronouncing the Waaw Madd or the Yaa Madd from the nostrils with Ghunnah. To correct this mistake, pinch your nose and say the Madd letter; if the sound becomes muted whilst pinching your nose, or if it sounds like one has a cold, it is indeed coming through the nose, and is therefore incorrect. The sound needs to be focused and pronounced through the mouth.

Example: يَفْعَلُونَ

The Throat

There are three points of articulation in the throat and each point has two letters emitted from therein. Each point of articulation has two spots which produce different sounds.

1- The deepest part of the throat
2- The middle part of the throat
3- The closest part of the throat (closest to the mouth)

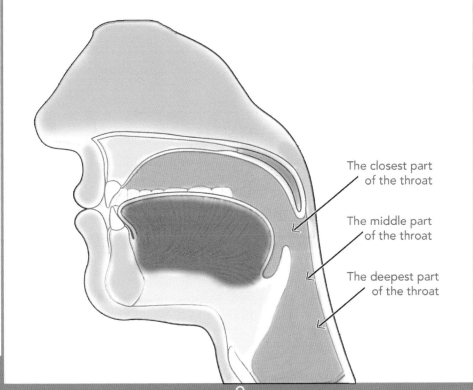

The closest part of the throat

The middle part of the throat

The deepest part of the throat

The Throat

The Makhraj of the throat letters

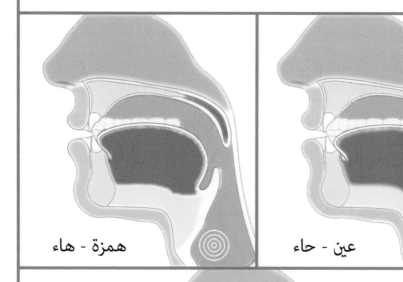

همزة - هاء

عين - حاء

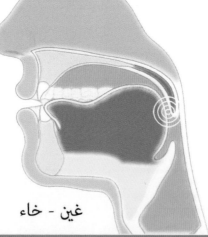

غين - خاء

The Throat

The deepest part of the throat:

هاء - همزة

These letters are pronounced from the deepest part of the throat which is the furthest away from the mouth and the closest to the chest. (1)

The middle part of the throat:

عين - حاء

These letters are pronounced from the middle part of the throat which lies half way in between the beginning and the end of the throat. (2)

The closest part of the throat:

غين - خاء

These letters are pronounced from the closest part of the throat which is the beginning of the throat, or the closest to the mouth. (3)

Note (1): The English (H) is pronounced at a position higher in the throat than the Arabic هاء

(2): The two letters pronounced from the middle of the throat are not in the English language so you need some practice to succeed in pronouncing them correctly. The first step is to get used to using this part of the throat. Think of the throat squeezing against itself from the middle, and try to pronounce the letters from that point. Listening to a Quran reciter and trying to copy his pronunciation will work well insha'Allah.

(3) You should practice using this part of the throat, غين is pronounced from the area used for gargling, خاء is pronounced from an area deeper than the قاف

The Throat

Common mistakes:

1- Pronouncing the همزة heavy, it should always be light.
Example: أَصَابَهُمْ

2- Not pronouncing the همزة clearly when stopping on it at the end of a word.
Example: السَّمَاءُ

3- Pronouncing the هاء heavy, it should always be light.
Example: النَّهَارِ

4- Not pronouncing the هاء clearly when it is preceded by هاء or حاء.
Examples: جِبَاهُهُمْ - وَسَبِّحْهُ

5- Not pronouncing the هاء clearly when stopping on it at the end of a word.
Example: فَعَلُوهُ

6- Pronouncing the عين as if it is همزة.
Example: يَعْلَمُونَ

7- Pronouncing the عين heavy, it should always be light.
Example: عَصَوْا

The Throat

Common mistakes:

8- Pronouncing the غين as if it is قاف.

Example: غَيْرِ الْمَغْضُوبِ

9- Exaggerating the heaviness of the غين when it has Kasrah.

Example: مِنْ غِلٍّ

10- Pronouncing the خاء light, it should always be heavy.

Example: خَالِدِينَ

11- Exaggerating the heaviness of the خاء when it has Kasrah.

Example: خِيفَةً

12- Pronouncing the حاء as if it is هاء.

Example: الْحَمْدُ

The Tongue

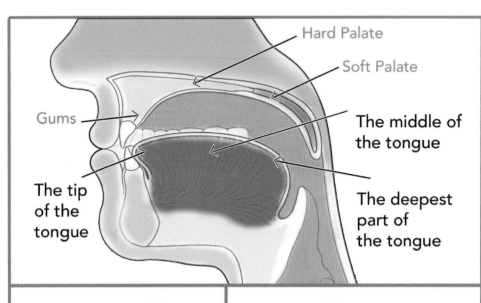

Hard Palate

Soft Palate

Gums

The middle of the tongue

The tip of the tongue

The deepest part of the tongue

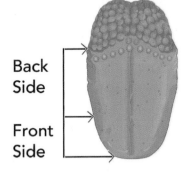

Back Side

Front Side

The edges (sides) of the tongue

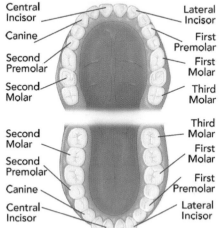

Central Incisor

Lateral Incisor

Canine

First Premolar

Second Premolar

First Molar

Second Molar

Third Molar

Second Molar

Third Molar

Second Premolar

First Molar

Canine

First Premolar

Central Incisor

Lateral Incisor

The Tongue

There are ten articulation points for eighteen letters. These ten articulation points are distributed over four areas of the tongue:
1- The deepest part of the tongue.
2- The middle of the tongue.
3- The edges (sides) of the tongue.
4- The tip of the tongue.

The roof of the mouth is divided into 2 parts:
- The hard palate; the top roof area, near the teeth.
- The soft palate; deepest part of the roof, near the throat.
The tongue touches the gums or the hard or the soft palates to produce different letters.

Areas of the tongue		Letters
Deepest part	1	قاف
	2	كاف
Middle part	3	جيم - شين - ياء
Edges	4	لام
	5	ضاد
Tip	6	نون
	7	راء
	8	تاء - دال - طاء
	9	سين - زاي - صاد
	10	ثاء - ذال - ظاء

The deepest part of the tongue

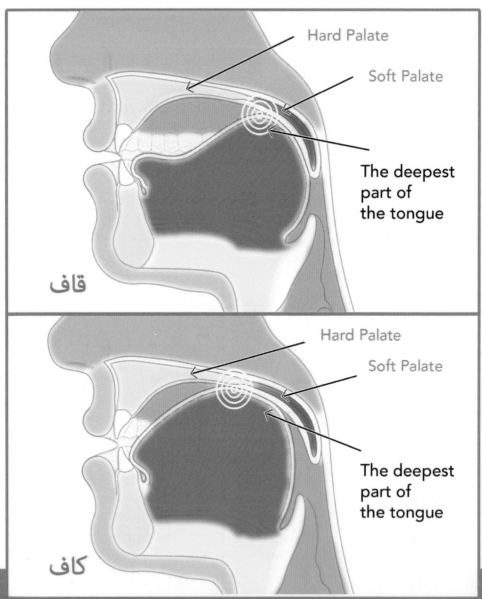

Hard Palate

Soft Palate

The deepest
part of
the tongue

قاف

Hard Palate

Soft Palate

The deepest
part of
the tongue

كاف

The deepest part of the tongue

قاف

This letter is articulated from the deepest part of the tongue and what lies opposite, which is the roof of the mouth in the area of the soft palate.

كاف

This letter is articulated from the deepest part of the tongue and what lies opposite, which is the roof of the mouth in the area of the hard palate. This letter is closer to the mouth than the قاف.

Common mistakes:

1- Changing the قاف to كاف and the كاف to قاف

Example: قَلْبٌ – كَلْبٌ

2- Pronouncing the قاف light when it has Kasrah.

Example: الْحَقِّ

3- Pronouncing the كاف heavy when it is preceded by a heavy letter.

Example: صَدْرُكَ

4- Excessive air whilst pronouncing the قاف.

Example: قَبْلَكَ

17

The Middle of the Tongue

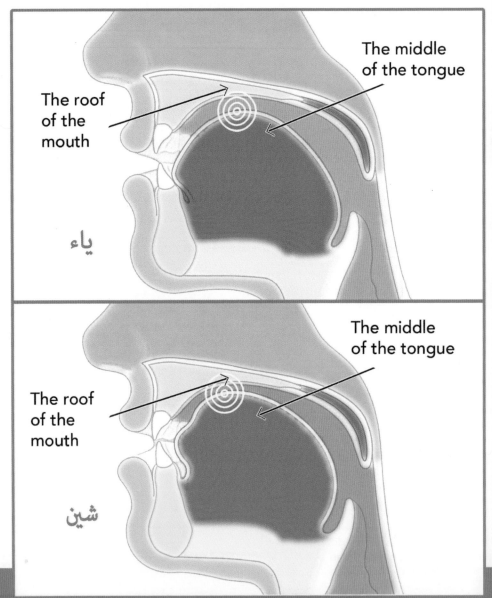

The roof of the mouth

The middle of the tongue

ياء

The roof of the mouth

The middle of the tongue

شين

The Middle of the Tongue

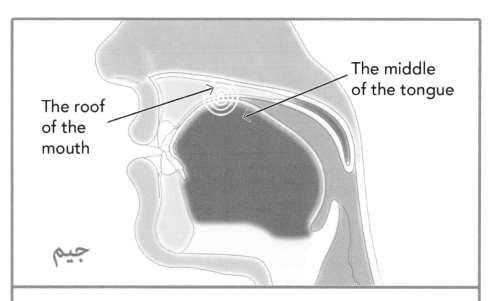

The middle of the tongue

The roof of the mouth

جيم

جيم - شين - ياء

These three letters are pronounced from the middle of the tongue and what lies opposite, which is the roof of the mouth. (1)

This Yaa is not the Yaa Madd.

Note (1): There is a difference between the pronunciation of the Arabic جيم وشين and the English (j and sh). The English (j) and (sh) are pronounced from the front of the tongue and the hard palate.

The Middle of the Tongue

Common mistakes:

1- Pronouncing the جِيم like شِين.

Example: الْمُجْتَهِدِينَ

2- Not making Qalqalah when pronouncing the جِيم.

Example: يَجْمَعُونَ

3- Pronouncing the شِين from the tip of the tongue and making it sounds similar to the سِين.

Example: مِنَ الشَّيْطَانِ

4- Pronouncing the شِين heavy when it is followed by a heavy letter.

Example: شَطَطًا

5- Excessive air whilst pronouncing the يَاء.

Example: عَلَيْهِمْ

The Sides of the Tongue

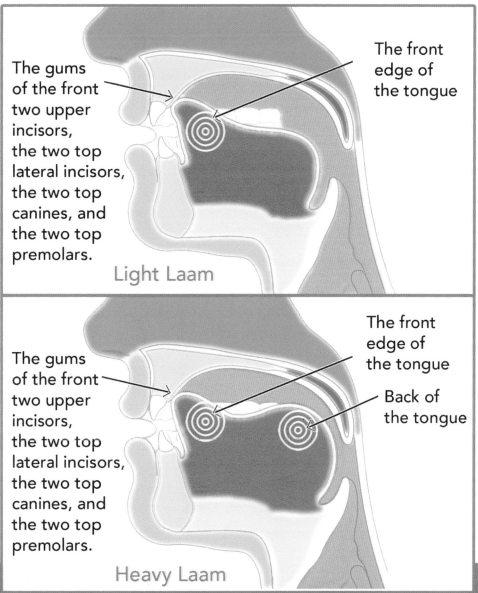

The gums
of the front
two upper
incisors,
the two top
lateral incisors,
the two top
canines, and
the two top
premolars.

The front
edge of
the tongue

Light Laam

The gums
of the front
two upper
incisors,
the two top
lateral incisors,
the two top
canines, and
the two top
premolars.

The front
edge of
the tongue

Back of
the tongue

Heavy Laam

The Sides of the Tongue

لام

This letter is pronounced from the front sides and the tip of the tongue touching what lies opposite to them, which are the gums of the two top front incisors, the two top lateral incisors, the two top canines, and the two top premolars. (1)

To pronounce the heavy Lam, the reciter should raise the back of the tongue towards the upper palate.

Common mistakes:

1- Pronouncing the لام from the tip of the tongue.

Example: بَلْ

2- Making Idghaam for the لام and the following letter, especially when it is followed by نون as the point of articulation of the نون is close to that of the لام.

Example: أَنزَلْنَاهُ

3- Pronouncing the لام heavy where it should be light.

Examples: اللَّطِيفُ — عَلَى اللَّهِ

4- Making Qalaqalah when pronouncing لام Saakin.

Examples: الْكِتَابُ

Note (1): There is a difference between the pronunciation of the Arabic لم and the English (l), the English (l) is pronounced by placing the tip of the tongue on the roof of the mouth, just behind the teeth.

The Sides of the Tongue

ضاد

This letter is pronounced from one or both back sides of the tongue touching the molars and the gum area next to the molars.

Common mistakes:

1- Using the tip of the tongue and the gums of the two front teeth to pronounce the ضاد instead of the back sides of the tongue, it will sound like a heavy دال.

Example: تُفِيضُونَ

2- Making Qalqalah.

Example: وَقَضْبًا

3- Using the tip of the tongue and the edges of the two front teeth, it will sound like ظاء

Example: الضَّالِّينَ

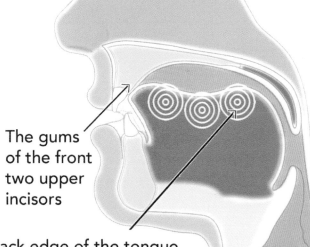

The gums of the front two upper incisors

The back edge of the tongue

23

The Tip of the Tongue

نون

This letter is pronounced from the tip of the tongue and the gums of the front two upper incisors, نون is pronounced slightly behind the gums (towards the upper palate) in comparison to the articulation point of the لام. Part of the sound comes from the mouth whilst the other part comes from the nose.

Common mistakes:

1- Not pronouncing the نون clearly when stopping on it at the end of a word.

Example: نَسْتَعِينُ

2-Making Qalqalah when the نون is Sakinah.

Example: أَنْعَمْتَ

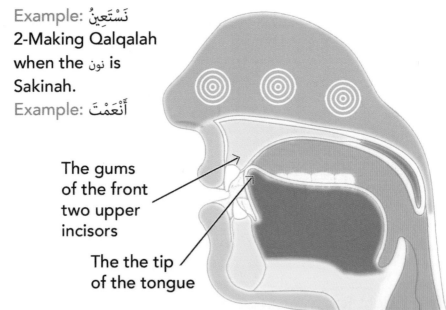

The gums of the front two upper incisors

The the tip of the tongue

The Tip of the Tongue

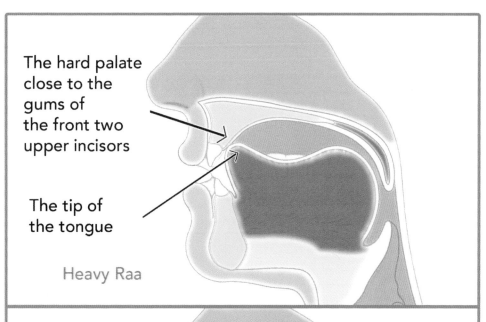

The hard palate close to the gums of the front two upper incisors

The tip of the tongue

Heavy Raa

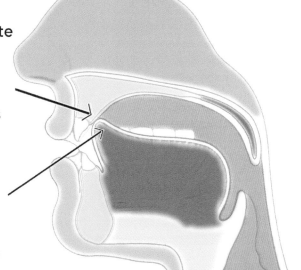

The hard palate close to the gums of the front two upper incisors

The tip of the tongue

Light Raa

The Tip of the Tongue

راء

This letter is pronounced from the tip of the tongue and the hard palate close to the gums of the front two upper incisors. There should be no trilling of the tongue when pronouncing this letter. One should physically feel the tongue hit the gums of the two upper front incisors, as the English (r) is pronounced without the tongue striking the gums of the front two upper incisors.

Leaving a small space for the sound to run at the very tip of the tongue will help to pronounce the راء correctly.

Common mistakes:

1- Trilling of the tongue whilst pronouncing the letter which causes the letter to be pronounced multiple times.

Example: الرَّزَّاقُ

2- Making Dhammah whilst pronouncing the heavy راء.

Examples: الرَّحْمَنِ الرَّحِيمِ

3- Not pronouncing the الراء clearly when stopping on it at the end of a word.

Examples: خُسْرٌ - السِّحْرُ

The Tip of the Tongue

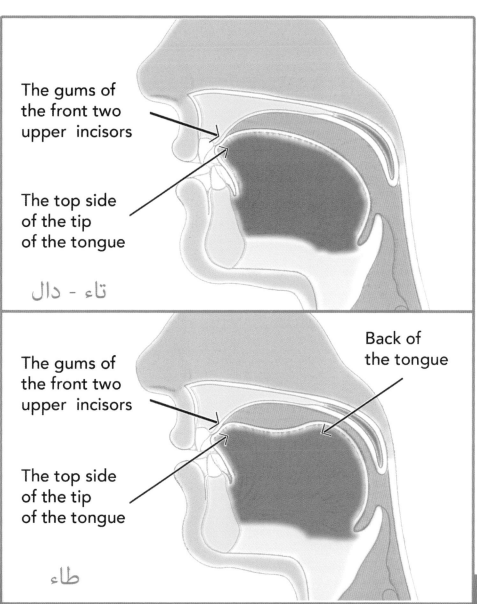

The gums of the front two upper incisors

The top side of the tip of the tongue

تاء - دال

The gums of the front two upper incisors

Back of the tongue

The top side of the tip of the tongue

طاء

The Tip of the Tongue

طاء - دال - تاء

These letters are pronounced from the top side of the tip of the tongue and the gums of the front two upper incisors, (further to the inside of the mouth). The back of the tongue is raised towards the upper palate to pronounce طاء.(1)

Common mistakes:

1- Pronouncing the طاء light.

Example: فَطَالَ

2- Pronouncing the دال heavy.

Example: صُدُورِ

3- Pronouncing the تاء heavy.

Example: تَطْمَئِنُّ

4- Pronouncing the دال as if it is تاء.

Example: الدِّينُ

5- Not making Qalqalah when pronouncing the طاء.

Example: أَطْعَمَهُمْ

6- Excessive air whilst pronouncing the تاء - دال - طاء.

Example: الطَّلَاقُ - والتِّينِ - دِينِ

Note (1): There is a difference between the pronunciation of the Arabic تاء & دال and the English (t & d), The English (t & d) are pronounced from the tip of the tongue touching the gums of the front teeth which makes the sound slightly heavy with excessive breath.

The Tip of the Tongue

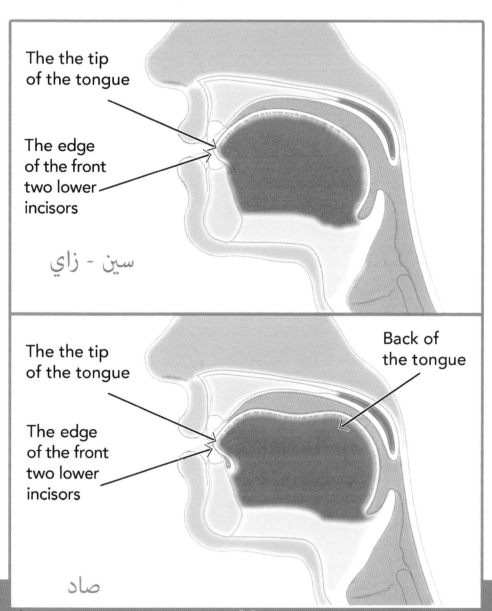

The the tip of the tongue

The edge of the front two lower incisors

سين - زاي

The the tip of the tongue

The edge of the front two lower incisors

Back of the tongue

صاد

The Tip of the Tongue

صاد - سين - زاي

These letters are pronounced from the tip of the tongue and the edge of the front two lower incisors. A whistle sound should be heard when pronouncing these letters. The back of the tongue is raised towards the upper palate to pronounce صاد. (1)

Common mistakes:

1- Pronouncing the صاد light.

Example: الْمَصِيرُ

2- Making Dhammah while pronouncing the صاد.

Example: الصَّالِحِينَ

3- Pronouncing the سين heavy.

Example: يَسْطُرُونَ

4- Pronouncing the سين as if it is زاي.

Example: وَاسْجُدْ

5- Pronouncing the زاي as if it is سين.

Example: إِذَا زُلْزِلَتِ

Note (1): There is a difference between the pronunciation of the Arabic زاي & سين and the English (s & z), The English (s & z) are pronounced from the tip of the tongue touching the gums of the front teeth.

The Tip of the Tongue

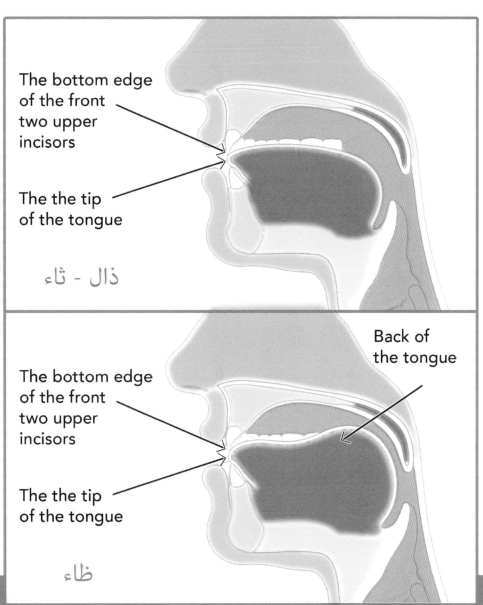

The bottom edge of the front two upper incisors

The the tip of the tongue

ذال - ثاء

Back of the tongue

The bottom edge of the front two upper incisors

The the tip of the tongue

ظاء

The Tip of the Tongue

ظاء - ذال - ثاء

These letters are pronounced from the tip of the tongue and the bottom edge of the front two upper incisors. The back of the tongue is raised towards the upper palate to pronounce ظاء.

Common mistakes:

1- Changing the ذال to زاي.

Example: وَالذَّاكِرِينَ

2- Changing the ثاء to سين.

Example: فَكَثَّرَكُمْ

3- Not pronouncing the ظاء heavy.

Example: الظَّالِمِينَ

The Lips

There are two articulation points for four letters.
The first point of articulation is for the فاء, the other one
is for the باء ، ميم ، واو.

فاء

The bottom edge of the front two upper incisors touches
the inner bottom lip.

Common mistakes:

1- The front two upper
incisors touching the
bottom lip lightly.

Example: تَفْعَلُونَ

2- Changing
the فاء to V.

Example: وَالضَّفَادِعَ

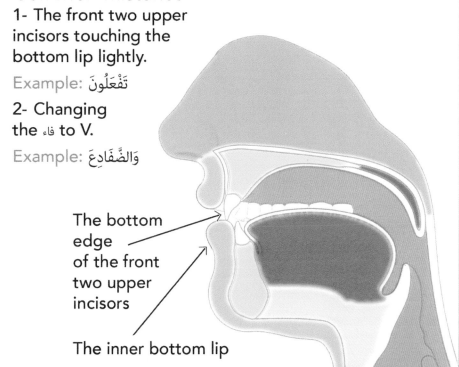

The bottom
edge
of the front
two upper
incisors

The inner bottom lip

33

The Lips

واو

Circling of the two lips without meeting completely.

This Waaw is not the Waaw Madd.

Common mistakes:

Pronouncing the واو heavy when followed by a heavy letter.

Example: وَاللَّه

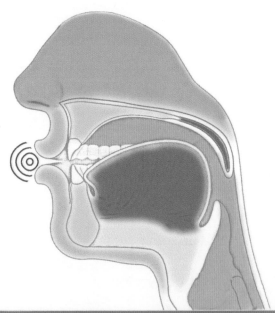

The Lips

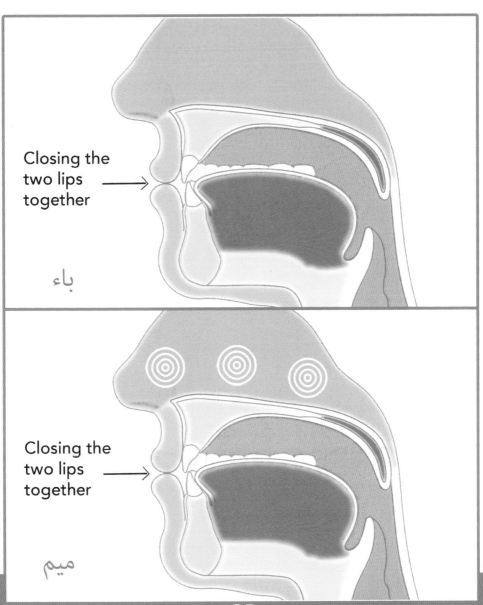

Closing the two lips together

باء

Closing the two lips together

ميم

The Lips

باء - ميم

Closing the two lips together.

When pronouncing the ميم , part of the sound comes from the mouth whilst the other part comes from the nose.

Common mistakes:

1- Pronouncing the باء heavy when followed by a heavy letter.

Example: البَاطِلِ

2- Not making Qalqalah when pronouncing the باء.

Example: يُبْصِرُونَ

3- Pronouncing the ميم heavy.

Example: مَخْمَصَةٍ

4- Making Qalqalah when pronouncing the ميم.

Example: يَمْتَرُونَ

The Nasal Cavity

نون – ميم

It is a large air-filled space above and behind the nose in the middle of the face. Each cavity is the continuation of one of the two nostrils. There is one articulation point, that of the Ghunnah.

Ghunnah is a characteristic, not a letter. It is a characteristic of Meem and Noon letters.

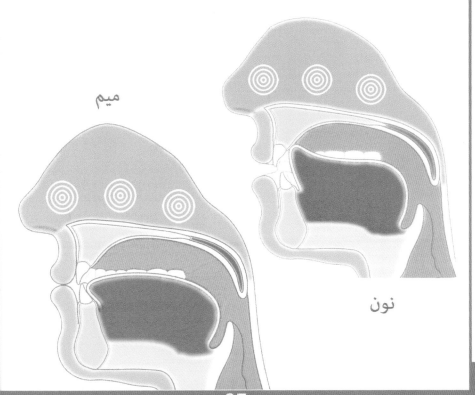

Third Section

Exercises

Jannat
Al Quran

Exercises

Makharij

1- Define the following:
   1- The articulation point
   2- The sound
   3- The letter

2- Find 2 common mistakes when pronouncing the following:
   1- The letters of Madd
   2- The throat letters
   3- قاف - كاف
   4- جيم - شين - ياء
   5- لام - ضاد
   6- راء - نون
   7- طاء - دال - تاء
   8- صاد - سين - زاي
   9- ظاء - ذال - ثاء
   10- باء - ميم

3- How to know whether you are pronouncing the Waaw Madd or the Yaa Madd from the nostrils with Ghunnah?

4- What are the four areas of the tongue?

Exercises

Makharij

5- Complete the following:

1- Arabic is a unique language in which each letter has a certain ....

2- To know the point of articulation of any letter, put a .... before the letter.

3- There are .... major areas of the speech system that are used to pronounce the letters.

4- The empty space in the mouth and throat has one articulation point for the letters...................

5- The Throat has .... articulation points for six different letters.

6- The Tongue has .... articulation points for eighteen letters.

7- The Two Lips have .... articulation points for four letters.

8- همزة - هـاء are pronounced from .... part of the throat.

9- The roof of the mouth is divided into 2 parts which are .... & ....

10- لام is pronounced from .... touching what lies opposite to them, which are the gums of the two top front incisors, the two top lateral incisors, the two top canines, and the two top premolars.

Exercises

Makharij

5- Complete the following:

11- To pronounce the heavy Lam, the reciter...................

12- ضاد is pronounced from .... of the tongue touching the molars and the gum area next to the molars.

13- نون is pronounced from the .... of the tongue and what lies opposite, which is the gums of the front two upper incisors.

14- تاء is pronounced from the .... of the tongue and the gums of the front two upper incisors.

15- سين is pronounced from the tip of the tongue and the top edge of the front two .... incisors.

16- When pronouncing فا the bottom edge of the two upper front teeth touches ....

6- Put (✔) for the true statement and (✗) for the false statement and correct the mistake.

1- The Nasal Cavity is a large air-filled space above and behind the nose in the middle of the face. (   )

2- Waaw Sakinah preceded by a Dhammah is one of the letters of Madd. (   )

3- The three Madd letters have a specific place that they are pronounced from. (   )

Exercises

Makharij

6- Put (✔) for the true statement and (✘) for the false statement and correct the mistake.

4- The Madd letters are prolonged four harakahs if they are not followed by a hamzah or a sukoon. ( )

5- حاء & عين are pronounced from the deepest part of the throat. ( )

6- The English (H) is pronounced from the same position in the throat as the Arabic هاء ( )

7- غين is pronounced from the area used for gargling. ( )

8- قاف is articulated from the deepest part of the tongue and what lies opposite, which is the roof of the mouth in the area of the hard palate. ( )

9- There is no difference between the pronunciation of the Arabic جيم وشين and the English (j and sh). ( )

10- There is a difference between the pronunciation of the Arabic لام and the English (l), the English (l) is pronounced by placing the tip of the tongue on the roof of the mouth, just behind the teeth. ( )

11- There should be a trilling of the tongue when pronouncing راء. ( )

Exercises

Makharij

6- Put (✔) for the true statement and (✘) for the false statement and correct the mistake.

12- The back of the tongue is raised towards the upper palate to make طاء heavy. (   )

13- A whistle sound should be heard when pronouncing the زاي. (   )

14- ذال is pronounced from the tip of the tongue and the bottom edges of the front two lower incisors. (   )

15- واو should be pronounced heavy when followed by a heavy letter. (   )

16- To pronounce صاد heavy, make Dhammah while pronouncing it. (   )

17- باء should be pronounced heavy when followed by a heavy letter. (   )

Fourth Section

The Qualities of the letters
(Sifaat) صِفَاتُ الْحُرُوفِ

The Permanent Qualities
with Opposites

The Permanent Qualities
Without Opposites

Jannat
Al Quran

The Qualities of the letters
(Sifaat) صِفَاتُ الْحُرُوفِ

It is the method in which a letter is articulated that differentiates it from other letters. The purpose of these characteristics is to distinguish the letters that share the same articulation points (Makhaarij). These characteristics are clear when the letter has Sukoon.

Makhaarij only provides information as to where the sound of the letter comes from, whereas Sifaat provides extra information with regards to the characteristics of the letter in order to produce the correct sound.

The letters have two types of qualities:
1- Permanent qualities: These are the characteristics that are part of the fundamental make-up of the letter, the letter cannot be pronounced correctly without this quality. Permanent qualities are covered in this lesson.

2- Presented qualities: These are characteristics which are present in a letter in some cases such as Izhaar or Idghaam. Presented qualities are not covered in this lesson.

The Qualities of the letters
(Sifaat) صِفَاتُ الْحُرُوفِ

The Permanent Qualities with Opposites:

1	Al-Hams الْهَمْسُ	Al-Jahr الْجَهْرُ
2	Ash-Shiddah الشَّدَّةُ	Ar-Rakhawa الرَّخَاوَةُ
	At-Tawassut or Al-Baineyyah - التَّوَسُّطُ الْبَيْنِيَّةُ	
3	Al-Istilaa الاسْتِعْلَاءُ	Al-Istifaal الاسْتِفَالُ
4	Al-Itbaaq الْإِطْبَاقُ	Al-Infitah الانْفِتَاحُ
5	Al-Idhlaq الْإِذْلَاقُ	Al-Ismat الْإِصْمَاتُ

The Permanent Qualities without Opposites:

1	Qalqalah الْقَلْقَلَةُ
2	As-Safeer الصَّفِيرُ
3	Al-Leen اللِّينُ
4	Al-Inhiraf الانْحِرَافُ
5	At-Takreer التَّكْرِيرُ
6	At-Tafashy التَّفَشِّي
7	Al-Istitaalah الاسْتِطَالَةُ
8	Al-Ghunnah الْغُنَّةُ

Every letter has at least five permanent qualities that are always associated with it. A letter can never have both opposite qualities.

Some letters have qualities without opposites.

The Permanent Qualities with Opposites

1- Al-Hams الْهَمْسُ

Literal meaning is whispering.

Technical meaning is the continuation of the breath when pronouncing the letter, due to weakness at its point of articulation.

The following letters have this quality:

فحثه شخص سكت

Examples:

بِسْمِ ٱللَّهِ ٱلرَّحْمَـٰنِ ٱلرَّحِيمِ - أَكْثَرَهُمْ - تَتْلُوا

Al-Jahr الْجَهْرُ

Literal meaning is to be apparent.

Technical meaning is the discontinuation of the breath when pronouncing the letter, due to strength at its point of articulation.

The rest of the letters have this quality.

Examples:

وَإِذْ قَالَ - طَغْيَانِهِمْ

The Permanent Qualities with Opposites

2- Ash-Shiddah الشِّدَّةُ

Literal meaning is strength.

Technical meaning is the discontinuation of the sound when pronouncing the letter, due to strength at its point of articulation.

The following letters have this quality:

أجد قط بكت

There are Jahr, Shiddah & Qalqalah in these letters:

قطب جد

There are Hams & Shiddah in these letters: كاف - تاء (1)

There are Jahr & Shiddah in this letter: همزة

Examples: سُطِحَتْ - الْحَقُّ - يُؤْمِنُونَ

At-Tawassut or Al-Baineyyah - التَّوَسُّطُ الْبَيْنِيَّةُ

Literal meaning is moderation.

Technical meaning is that the sound of the letter is neither cut off nor allowed to continue.

The following letters have this quality: لن عمر

The sound of these letters starts at a point of articulation then stops and continues to be heard in another point of articulation except the letter عين.

Note (1): The sound of the letter stops and then the breath is released.

The Permanent Qualities with Opposites

At-Tawassut or Al-Baineyyah - التَّوَسُّطُ الْبَيْنِيَّةُ

نون

The sound starts when the tip of the tongue touches what lies opposite to it, which is the gums of the front two upper incisors, and the sound continues to be heard in the nasal cavity before it stops.

Example: أَنْعَمْتَ

ميم

The sound starts by closing the two lips together and the sound continues to be heard in the nasal cavity before it stops.

Examples: لَمْ - الْحَمْدُ

عين

This letter is pronounced from the middle part of the throat, then the sound stops.

Examples: يَعْمَلُونَ

The Permanent Qualities with Opposites

At-Tawassut or Al-Baineyyah - التَّوَسُّطُ الْبَيْنِيَّةُ

لام

The sound starts when the front sides and the tip of the tongue touch what lies opposite to them which are the gums of the two top front incisors, the two top lateral incisors, the two top canines, and the two top premolars. Then the sound deviates to the back sides of the tongue before it stops.

Example: في الْبِلَادِ - الْقُرْءَانَ

الراء

The sound starts when the tip of the tongue touches the hard palate close to the gums of the front two upper incisors, then the sound deviates to the middle part of the tip of the tongue before it stops.

Example: يَرْفَعُ - الْفُرْقَانَ

The Permanent Qualities with Opposites

Ar-Rakhawa الرَّخَاوَةُ

Literal meaning is softness.

Technical meaning is the continuation of the sound when pronouncing the letter, due to weakness at its point of articulation.

All letters other than the letters of Shiddah and Tawassut have this quality.

Notes regarding the timing of the letters:

1- The letters that are Saakinah and have Rakhawa are equal in timing.

Example: نَشْرَحْ - أَضْطَرُّهُ

2- The letters that are Saakinah and have Baineyyah are equal in timing.

Example: وَانْحَرْ

3- The letters that are Saakinah and have Shiddah are equal in timing.

Example: مَطْلَعِ الْفَجْرِ

4- The timing of the letters that have Rakhawa is longer than that of the letters that have Baineyyah.

Example: أَلَمْ نَشْرَحْ

The Permanent Qualities with Opposites

Ar-Rakhawa الرَّخَاوَةُ

Notes regarding the timing of the letters:

5- The timing of the letters that have Baineyyah is longer than that of the letters that have Shiddah.

Example: وَوَضَعْنَا عَنكَ وِزْرَكَ

6- The timing of all the letters that have Harakahs are the same.

The timing of the letter that has Fathah = The timing of the letter that has Dammah = The timing of the letter that has Kasrah.

Examples: كُتِبَ — يَعِظُكُمْ — سُئِلَتْ

Common mistakes:

1- Prolonging the timing of the Harakah. It is called Tamteet تَمْطِيطٌ.

Example (1): فَمَن يَعْمَلْ

Wrong pronunciation: فَمَان يَعْمَلْ

Example (2): كُنتُمْ

Wrong pronunciation: كُونتُمْ

Example (3): إِنَّ الَّذِينَ

Wrong pronunciation: إِينَ الَّذِينَ

2- Shortening the timing of the Harakah. It is called Ikhtilas إِخْتِلَاسٌ.

Examples: يَأْمُرُكُمْ — خَلَقَكُمْ - يَعِدُكُمْ

The Permanent Qualities with Opposites

3- Al-Istilaa الِاسْتِعْلَاءُ

Literal meaning is elevation.

Technical meaning is the elevation of the back of the tongue towards the roof of the mouth when pronouncing a letter.

The following letters have this quality: خص ضغط قظ

Example: الطَّلَاقُ - قَالَ - الظَّالِمِينَ - أَغْطَشَ - يَضْرِبُ - صِبْغَةَ - صَدَقَ

Al-Istifaal الِاسْتِفَالُ

Literal meaning is lowering or dropping.

Technical meaning is keeping the back of the tongue lowered from the roof of the mouth whilst pronouncing a letter.

All letters other than the letters of Istilaa are letters of Istifaal.

These letters are the light letters, pronounced with an empty mouth.

Example: والتِّينِ - الْكِتَابُ

The Permanent Qualities with Opposites

4- Al-Itbaaq الْإِطْبَاق

Literal meaning is adhesion.

Technical meaning is adhesion of a large part of the tongue to the roof of the mouth whilst pronouncing the letter.

The following letters have this quality: ظ ط ض ص

Note: The letters that have Itbaaq must have Istilaa.

Examples: فَطَالَ - الصِّرَاطَ - الظَّالِمِينَ - ضَلَالٍ

Al-Infitah الِانْفِتَاح

Literal meaning is separation.

Technical meaning is that there is a gap between a large part of the tongue and the roof of the mouth whilst pronouncing the letter.

All letters other than that of Itbaaq are letters of Infitah.

Example: صُدُورِ

The Permanent Qualities with Opposites

				Levels of Heaviness:			
From the strongest to the weekest	طاء	ضاد	ظاء	صاد	قاف	غين	خاء
The letter has Fathah followed by Alif	طَابَ	ضَاق	تَظَاهَرُونَ	صَالِحَ	يُقَاتِلُونَ	الْغَاشِيَةُ	خَابَ
The letter has Fathah not followed by Alif	طَبَع	ضَرَب	ظَلَمَ	صَرَف	قَتَل	غَفَر	خَلَق
The letter has Dammah	طُبِعَ	ضُرِبَتْ	ظُلِمَ	صُرِفَتْ	قُتِل	غُلِبَتْ	خُلِقَ
The letter is Saakin	يَطْبَعُ	يُضْلِلُ	يَظْلِمُ	يَصْرِفْهُ	يَقْتُل	مَغْفِرَةٍ	يَخْلُقُ
The letter has Kasrah	طِبَاقًا	ضِرَارًا	ظِلَالًا	صِرَاطًا	قِتَالٍ	غِلٌّ	خِفَافًا

The Permanent Qualities with Opposites

5- Al-Idhlaq الْإِذْلَاقُ

Literal meaning is fluency.

Technical meaning is the articulation of the letters with utmost ease from the sides of the tongue or lips.

The following letters have this quality: فر من لب

Note: You should find one or more of these letters in any four or five letter root words in the Arabic Language. If none of these letters are found in a four or five letter root word, then it is not an Arabic word.

Example: عَسْجَد
It is not an Arabic word.

Al-Ismat الْإِصْمَاتُ

Literal meaning is desisting or refusal.

Technical meaning is the articulation of the letters with utmost strength and stability from their Makhraaj.
All letters other than the letters of Al-Idhlaaq are letters of Al-Ismaat.

The Permanent Qualities Without Opposites

1. Qalqalah اَلْقَلْقَلَة

Literal meaning is vibration.

Technical meaning is making an echo or vibration at the articulation point of the letter if it has Sukoon on top of it or will be made Saakin because of stopping on that letter.

The following letters have this quality: قطب جد

Types of Qalqalah:

1- Minor (Sughra) قلقلة صغرى

This occurs when the letter of Qalqalah is in the middle of a word, or at the end of a word that you are not stopping on.

Examples: قَدْ قَالَهَا - يُطْعِمُونَ

2- Medium (Wusta) قلقلة وسطى

This occurs when the letter of Qalqalah is at the end of a word, the letter of Qalqalah does not have Shaddah, and you are stopping on that word.

Example: وَالطَّارِقِ

The Permanent Qualities Without Opposites

1. Qalqalah اَلْقَلْقَلَةُ

Types of Qalqalah:

3- Major (Kubra) قلقلة كبرى

This occurs when the letter of Qalqalah is at the end of a word, the letter of Qalqalah has Shaddah and you are stopping on that word.

Example: بِالْحَقِّ

The sound of the Major Qalqalah is clearer than that of the Meduim Qalqalah and the sound of the Medium Qalqalah is clearer than that of the Minor Qalqalah.

Common mistakes:

1- Pronouncing the Qalqalah with Harakah.

Example: لَقَدْ كَانَ

Wrong pronunciation: لَقَدَ كَانَ

2- Pronouncing the Qalqalah with Hamza.

Example: أَحَدْ

3- Not pronouncing the Qalqalah clear enough.

Example: يَدْخُلُونَ

The Permanent Qualities Without Opposites

2. As-Safeer الصَّفِيرُ

Literal meaning **is a whistle.**

Technical meaning **is hearing a whistle whilst pronouncing the letters because the air emitted passes through a narrow passage. It is a natural sound that is produced when you pronounce the Safeer letters from the correct Makhraaj.**

The following letters have this quality: سين - صاد - زاي

Examples: وِزْرَكَ — الْمِسْكِينُ - سَيَصْلَى

3. Al-Leen اللِّينُ

Literal meaning **is easiness and softness.**

Technical meaning **is pronouncing the letters of Leen from its Makhraaj with a natural ease and softness, and having the ability to prolong the Leen letters similar to prolonging the letters of Madd, when you stop on the letter following them.**

The following letters have this quality: واو - ياء

Examples: بَيْتٍ - خَوْفٍ

The Permanent Qualities
Without Opposites

4. Al-Inhiraf الإنْحِرَافُ

Literal meaning is deviation.

Technical meaning is that the sound starts at one point of articulation then deviates to another point of articulation.

The following letters have this quality: لام — راء

When pronouncing the لام , the sound starts when the front sides and the tip of the tongue touch what lies opposite to them, which are the gums of the two top front incisors, the two top lateral incisors, the two top canines, and the two top premolars. Then the sound deviates to the back sides of the tongue.

When pronouncing the راء , the sound starts when the tip of the tongue touches the hard palate close to the gums of the front two upper incisors, and then the sound deviates to the middle part of the tip of the tongue.

Examples: وَأَرْسَلَ - وَالْفَتْحِ

The Permanent Qualities Without Opposites

5. At-Takreer التَّكْرِيرُ

Literal meaning is repetition.

Technical meaning is the trilling of the tongue whilst pronouncing the letter which causes it to be pronounced multiple times.

The reciter should avoid repetition of the letter. The benefit of this quality is to know the Makhraaj of the letter.

The following letter has this quality: راء

Example: الْأَرْضُ

6. At-Tafashy التَّفَشِّي

Literal meaning is spreading and expansion.

Technical meaning is spreading the sound of the letter starting from the middle of the tongue and the upper palate until it reaches the front part of the tongue.

The following letter has this quality: شين

Examples: والشَّمْسِ

The Permanent Qualities
Without Opposites

7. Al-Istitaalah الاِسْتِطَالَةُ

Literal meaning is prolongation.

Technical meaning is the prolongation of the sound throughout its Makhraj until it reaches the front edge of the tongue (The Makhraj of Lam).

The following letter has this quality: ضاد

Example: تَضْلِيلٍ

8. Al-Ghunnah الْغُنَّةُ

Literal meaning is a sound that is emitted from the nasal passage.

Technical meaning is a sound that accompanies the pronunciation of ميم & نون when they have Sukoon, Harakah or Shaddah.

The following letters have this quality: نون & ميم

Examples: إِنَّ – مَن تَابَ – لَنَا
أَمَّا – فَاحْكُم بِيْنَهُمْ – مَا

The Permanent Qualities Without Opposites

	8. Al-Ghunnah الْغُنَّة			
Levels of Ghunnah:				
	Most Complete Ghunnah	Complete Ghunnah	Incomplete Ghunnah	Most Incomplete Ghunnah
Level	Longest Ghunnah	Second longest Ghunnah	This Ghunnah is shorter in timing than the complete Ghunnah	This is the shortest Ghunnah of all
Cases	1- Noon & Meem that have Shaddah 2- Complete & incomplete Idghaam	1- Ikhfaa 2- Ikhaa Shafawi 3- Iqlaab	Izhaar for Noon Saakin, Tanween & Meem Saakin	Noon & Meem that have Harakah Note: The time here is the time of Harakah
Examples for نون	إِنَّ - مِن نِعْمَةٍ مِن وَّالٍ - مَن يَشَاءُ - مِن مَّالٍ	مَن تَابَ - رِيحًا صِرْصَرًا - مِن بَعْدِ	أَنْعَمْتَ - سَمِيعٌ عَلِيمٌ	لَنَا
Examples for ميم	أَمَّا - هُم مِّنْ	فَاحْكُم بَيْنَهُمْ	لَمْ يَكُن	مَا

Fifth Section

Strong & Weak Qualities

Summary

Jannat
Al Quran

Strong & Weak Qualities

Some of the mentioned qualities are strong, weak or cannot be described by weakness or heaviness.

Qualities:

Strong	Weak	Cannot be described by weakness or heaviness
1- Al- Jahr الْجَهْرُ 2- Ash-Shiddah الشِّدَّةُ 3- Al-Istilaa الِاسْتِعْلَاءُ 4- Al-Itbaaq الْإِطْبَاقُ 5- Qalqalah الْقَلْقَلَةُ 6- As-Safeer الصَّفِيرُ 7- Al-Inhiraf الِانْحِرَافُ 8- At-Takreer التَّكْرِيرُ 9- At-Tafashy التَّفَشِّي 10- Al-Istitaalah الِاسْتِطَالَةُ 11- Al-Ghunnah الْغُنَّةُ	1- Al-Hams الْهَمْسُ 2- Ar-Rakhawa الرَّخَاوَةُ 3- Al-Istifaal الِاسْتِفَالُ 4- Al-Infitah الِانْفِتَاحُ 5- Al-Leen اَللِّينُ	1- Al-Idhlaq الْإِذْلَاقُ 2- Al-Ismat الْإِصْمَاتُ 3- At-Tawassut or Al-Baineyyah- الْبَيْنِيَّةُ – التَّوَسُّطُ

Strong & Weak Qualities

If most of the qualities of a letter are strong then this letter is strong, and if most of the qualities of a letter are weak then this letter is weak.

- The strongest letter is طاء as all its qualities are strong.

- Strong letter: It is the letter where most of its qualities are strong.
Example: صاد

- Moderate letter: It is the letter where its strong qualities are equal to its weak qualities.
Example: ميم

- Weak letter: It is the letter where most of its qualities are weak.
Example: ذال

- The weakest letters: It is the letter where all of its qualities are weak.
They are هاء & حاء

Summary

ض	ل	ي	ش	ج	ك	ق	خ	غ	ح	ع	ه	ء	ي	و	ا	Makhraj
edges		**middle part**		**deepest part**			**closest part**		**middle part**		**deepest part**		**Jawf**			
ض	ل	ي	ش	ج	ك	ق	خ	غ	ح	ع	ه	ء	ي	و	ا	Letter
✓	✓	✓		✓		✓		✓		✓		✓	✓	✓	✓	الْجَهْرُ
			✓		✓		✓		✓		✓					الْهَمْسُ
				✓	✓	✓						✓				الشِّدَّةُ
	✓									✓						الْبَيْنِيَّةُ
✓		✓	✓				✓	✓	✓		✓		✓	✓	✓	الرَّخَاوَةُ
✓						✓	✓	✓								الِاسْتِعْلَاءُ
	✓	✓	✓	✓	✓				✓	✓	✓	✓	✓	✓	✓	الِاسْتِفَالُ
✓																الْإِطْبَاقُ
	✓	✓	✓	✓	✓	✓	✓	✓	✓	✓	✓	✓	✓	✓	✓	الِانْفِتَاحُ
	✓															الْإِذْلَاقُ
✓		✓	✓	✓	✓	✓	✓	✓	✓	✓	✓	✓	✓	✓	✓	الْإِصْمَاتُ
				✓		✓										الْقَلْقَلَةُ
																الصَّفِيرُ
		✓														اللِّينُ
	✓															الِانْحِرَافُ
																التَّكْرِيرُ
			✓													التَّفَشِّي
✓																الِاسْتِطَالَةُ
																الْغُنَّةُ

Column groups: **Tongue** (ض, ل, ي, ش, ج, ك, ق) · **Throat** (خ, غ, ح, ع, ه, ء) · **Jawf** (ي, و, ا)

Summary

Lips				Tongue tip											Makhraj
و	ب	م	ف	ظ	ذ	ث	ص	ز	س	ط	د	ت	ر	ن	Letter
✓	✓	✓		✓	✓			✓		✓	✓		✓	✓	الْجَهْرُ
			✓			✓	✓		✓			✓			الْهَمْسُ
	✓									✓	✓	✓			الشِّدَّةُ
		✓											✓	✓	الْبَيْنِيَّةُ
✓			✓	✓	✓	✓	✓	✓	✓						الرَّخَاوَةُ
				✓			✓			✓					الاِسْتِعْلاءُ
✓	✓	✓	✓		✓	✓		✓	✓		✓	✓	✓	✓	الاِسْتِفَالُ
				✓			✓			✓					الإِطْبَاقُ
✓	✓	✓	✓		✓	✓		✓	✓		✓	✓	✓	✓	الاِنْفِتَاحُ
	✓	✓											✓	✓	الإِذْلاقُ
✓				✓	✓	✓	✓	✓	✓	✓	✓	✓			الإِصْمَاتُ
	✓									✓	✓				الْقَلْقَلَةُ
							✓	✓	✓						الصَّفِيرُ
✓															اللِّينُ
													✓		الاِنْحِرَافُ
													✓		التَّكْرِيرُ
															التَّفَشِّي
															الاِسْتِطَالَةُ
		✓												✓	الْغُنَّةُ

Sixth Section

Exercises

Jannat
Al Quran

Exercises

Sifaat

1- What is the purpose of learning Sifaat?

2- What information does Makharij and Sifaat provide?

3- What are the two types of Sifaat? Define them.

4- What are the levels of Qalqalah?

5- What are the levels of Ghunnah?

6- Complete the following:

   1- Every letter has at least .... permanent qualities that are always associated with it.

   2- ث & ذ have the same Makhraj, the qualities of .... & .... are common for these letters.

   3- Technical meaning of Ash-Shiddah is the .... of the sound when pronouncing the letter, due to strength at its point of articulation.

   4- The letters .... have Jahr, Shiddah & Qalqalah.

   5- The letters .... have Hams & Shiddah.

   6- The letter .... Has Jahr & Shiddah.

   7- When لام is pronounced the sound deviates to .... before if stops.

   8- When راء is pronounced the sound deviates to .... before if stops.

Exercises

Sifaat

6- Complete the following:

9- The mistake of prolonging the timing of the Harakah is called ....

10- The mistake of shortening the timing of the Harakah is called ....

11- The order of the heavy letters from the most heavy to the least heavy is: , ... , الظاء , ... , طاء الخاء , ..., القاف .

12- Technical meaning of As-Safeer is hearing a .... whilst pronouncing the letters.

13- Technical meaning of Al-Inhiraf is that ....

14- The benefit of the quality of Takreer is ....

15- The letters .... have Ghunnah.

16- The strongest letter is .... as all its qualities are strong.

7- Put (✔) for the true statement and (✘) for the false statement and correct the mistake.

1- A letter can have both opposite qualities and some letters have qualities without opposites. (   )

Exercises

Sifaat

7- Put (✔) for the true statement and (✘) for the false statement and correct the mistake.

2- Al-Hams is one of the qualities that doesn't have an opposite. ( )

3- ث is one of the letters that has Jahr. ( )

4- The sound of the letters that have Baineyyah starts at a point of articulation then stops and continues to be heard in another point of articulation except the letter عين. ( )

5- The letters that are Saakinah and have Rakhawa are equal in timing. ( )

6- The timing of the letters that have Rakhawa is longer than that of the letters that have Baineyyah. ( )

7- The timing of the letters that have Harakahs are different. ( )

8- Technical meaning of Istifaal is keeping the back of the tongue lowered from the roof of the mouth whilst pronouncing a letter. ( )

9- The letters that have Itbaaq must have Istilaa. ( )

10- عَسْجَد is an Arabic word. ( )

11- ضاد has the quality of Tafashy. ( )

12- Ar-Rakhawa is one of the strong Sifaat. ( )

13- As-Safeer is one of the weak Sifaat. ( )

Exercises

Sifaat

7- Write the Makhraj and Sifaat of the following letters:

1- ب

2- ت

3- ع

4- م

5- ض

6- ي

Printed in Great Britain
by Amazon